IN CELEBRATION OF

SUMMER

A Book of Seasonal Indulgences

IN CELEBRATION OF

SUM

MER

A Book of Seasonal Indulgences

BY HELEN THOMPSON

KODANSHA INTERNATIONAL

New York • Tokyo • London

For my mother, Louise Thompson, and my mother-in-law, Lavinia Lohrmann

Kodansha America, Inc.
114 Fifth Avenue, New York, New York 10011, U.S.A.

Kodansha International Ltd.
17-14 Otowa 1-chome, Bunkyo-ku, Tokyo 112, Japan

Published in 1998 by Kodansha America, Inc.

Library of Congress Cataloging-in-Publication Data

Thompson, Helen, 1948–
   In celebration of summer: a book of seasonal indulgences/by
  Helen Thompson; illustrator Carolyn Vibbert.
      p. cm.
  ISBN 1-56836-213-7
   1. Handicraft. 2. Cookery. 3. Summer—Miscellanea. I. Title.
TT157.T51523 1998
745.5—dc21   97-40562
                                               CIP

In Celebration of Summer is produced by becker&mayer!, Ltd.

Book design by Heidi Baughman and Trina Stahl
Cover illustration by Kristin Knutson
Interior illustrations by Carolyn Vibbert
Edited by Jennifer Worick

The *In Celebration* series also includes: *In Celebration of Spring,*
In Celebration of Autumn, and *In Celebration of Winter.*

Manufactured in Singapore on acid-free paper

98 99 00 01   10 9 8 7 6 5 4 3 2 1

Contents

Create a Bird Sanctuary

INCE THE WEATHER is warm and birds prefer to be outside, turn a secluded section of your yard into a bird sanctuary that offers shelter and sustenance. To create a feeding area, situate an open, shallow tray, box, or board on concrete blocks or flat rocks so that it sits about a foot off the ground; then place seed in bowls or spread it loosely on the feeding table. Encourage long-term bird sojourns at your sanctuary by planting berry-bearing shrubs and trees. Firethorn, cotoneaster, staghorn, sumac, mountain ash, winterberry holly, and eastern red cedar are a bird's idea of a feast. Other choices are Rocky Mountain juniper or American and fosteri hollies, which also provide good hideaways—as do evergreen trees and bushes. You'll get great pleasure from watching your avian guests enjoy your hospitality.

WHETHER YOU'RE AT THE BEACH, at the lake, or in the mountains, nightfall in summer often signals it's time to step outside again. Strike the perfect balance between whimsy and practicality, and light your evening activities with sturdy little oil lamps made from old doorknobs. These tiny beacons may sway in a sudden gust of wind but will then quickly right themselves again. And, since oil burns more hardily than wax, there's less of a chance they will blow out in a summer breeze than regular candles.

To find a suitable collection of old hollow doorknobs, scour junk shops, antique stores, and yard sales for elaborate brass, white enamel, or utilitarian metal knobs—all can be turned into clever miniature lamps to light up your night.

Project

DOORKNOB OIL LAMPS

hollow doorknobs

candlewicks

lamp oil

rivets

Clean and shine the knobs, and make sure the hollow parts are free of dirt and debris. Cut wicks to approximately 4 inches. Turn each knob upside down and fill the handle portion with oil. Thread the wick through the rivet, leaving 1 inch on one side and 3 inches on the other. Place the rivet on the upturned part of the knob, with the longer section of the wick submerged in oil. Arrange knobs in a cluster, and light each wick. After each use, trim the burned part of wick and pull another inch of clean wick through the rivet.

ARM SUMMER DAYS are meant to be spent in a garden, enjoying the fruits of your spring labors. Make it easier for yourself to step prettily among the flowers by creating a path of mosaic stepping-stones. Not only are these stones simple to make, they are a clever way to recycle cracked or broken dishes that you can't quite bear to throw away. If you're not in the habit of saving broken plates, consider using your oddments (though you'll have to break them in order to make the mosaics!) or look for plates at a garage or yard sale. Dinner plates with a central motif and a border design around the rim work best; if you don't have a plate with such a pattern, combine patterns from a plain dinner plate that has a border design and a dessert plate that has a central motif.

Project

MOSAIC STEPPING-STONES

dinner plates

heavy-duty grocery bags

garden gloves

11 ½-inch cement patio
    squares

hammer

newspaper

rubber gloves

particle mask

disposable measuring cups

water

2 disposable quart containers

1 ¼ pounds dry mortar

paint sticks

trowel or flat tool such
    as a ruler

old fork

1 ½ pounds dry exterior-
    grade grout

grout float or other smooth,
    flexible tool

damp cloth

soft cloth

sand

    After you have selected your plates, insert them one at a time into a grocery bag, face down so that the plate back rests against the folded bottom part of the bag, which will provide padding when you break the plate. Put on your garden gloves and set your packaged plate on the cement patio square. With the hammer, hit the plate hard several times. Open the bag gently to check the breakage—shards should be 1 ½ to 2 inches across. Repeat the process if you are also using a dessert plate.

On a piece of newspaper, trace the outline of the cement square. Still wearing gloves, tear the bag down the middle to expose the shards. Examine them and arrange the pieces from the border around the newsprint template, ½ inch from the edge. Reassemble the dessert plate motif in the center of the template. Move the shards closer together, adding extra pieces as needed. There should be about ⅛ to ¼ inch between shards.

Set the cement square on several sheets of newsprint. Don the rubber gloves and particle mask. Pour ½ cup cold water into a disposable container, add 1 ¾ cups dry mortar, and mix with a paint stick until thick. Let stand for 10 minutes, then pour onto the center of the square. With your trowel, spread the mortar over the surface about ¼ inch thick. To enhance adhesiveness, make grooves in the mortar with a fork. Move the shards, one by one, from the template to the square and press in gently; try to keep the surface even. Let the mosaic cure for a day.

To apply the grout, don rubber gloves and mask again. Pour ½ cup cold water in a disposable container and add 2 cups dry grout. Mix well until thick. Let stand 10 minutes and pour onto the center of the square. Smooth with the grout float until all the crevices are filled. Scrape off any excess with your hands. Let dry 10 minutes, then wipe the shards clean with a damp cloth. Let cure indoors for 72 hours. Buff with a soft cloth.

To set the stones in your garden, dig out a square shape about an inch larger and deeper than the stones. Layer the bottom with sand, and position the stones. Repeat process until path is complete. Water the area, and let the stones set. Then fill in the remaining gaps with dirt.

Makes approximately 15 stones

ANY OF THE WORLD'S greatest cocktails were meant to be imbibed languidly in a steamy climate, and such is the case with the Singapore Sling, invented at the legendary Raffles Hotel in Singapore. In colonial times, the hotel bar was a watering hole for the rich and famous, including Joseph Conrad, Somerset Maugham, and Douglas Fairbanks. Even if you don't have the luxury of dallying on a hotel terrace, you can at least enjoy a late afternoon respite as you sip this tropical mixture of gin, cherry brandy, and fruit. Add a touch of glamour by donning your best linen shirt and trousers, then find a place to lounge.

Project

THE SINGAPORE SLING

> *1 shot gin*
>
> *1 shot cherry brandy*
>
> *1 teaspoon sugar*
>
> *juice from ½ a lemon*
>
> *1 dash bitters*
>
> *ice*
>
> *collins glass*
>
> *soda or ginger ale*
>
> *lemon slice, orange slice, cherry (for garnish)*

For one Raffles Hotel Singapore Sling, combine the ingredients over ice in a collins glass, top with soda, and garnish with a slice of lemon, a slice of orange, and a cherry.

You may substitute ginger ale for soda, and some variations of the drink call for a shot of sloe gin or apricot brandy, a dash of port wine, Benedictine, Drambuie, or grenadine, in lieu of the cherry brandy.

Makes 1 sling

EMEMBER THE HOURS you spent as a child mean-
dering along a vast sweep of beach collecting
seashells? The shells themselves seemed like little gifts from the sea, variously and mysteriously curved,
and, if you held them close to your ear, able to echo the
roaring of the ocean. Or perhaps they were tiny and deli-
cately colored, too fragile to have emerged from the crash-
ing waves. If you have a collection of old shells from past
summer vacations, you can put them to new use as candle
holders. Seashell candles are an especially romantic way to
light a patio, deck, or screened porch, and a box of four
makes a pretty house gift.

Project
SHELL CANDLES

seashells (about 2 to 4
  inches across)

white craft glue

newspaper

old saucepan

cutting board

paring knife

wax, new candles, or
  candle stubs

old metal measuring cup

crayons (optional)

tongs

tweezers

wick (about 3 inches
  per shell)

scented oil (optional)

scissors (to snip off
  excess wicks)

artificial pearls

To make sure a seashell doesn't have cracks, fill it with water and check for leaks. To plug cracks, dry the shell and apply white craft glue to the outside of the crack. Let dry.

Place the newspaper on a kitchen counter near, but not too close to, the stove. Arrange the shells on this work surface, cavity-side up. In a saucepan, bring 1 inch of water to a boil. On the cutting board, slice the wax (either new or from old candle stubs) into ½-inch chunks. Place the chunks in an old metal measuring cup. If you are tinting the candles, add the crayons to the wax now. Then lower the cup into the boiling water with the tongs and reduce the heat to a simmer. Once the wax has melted, lift the cup out of the pan with the tongs, then pour hot wax into the cavity of one shell. Put the cup back into the saucepan.

With the tweezers, pick up a wick by one end, and press the other end into the hot wax until it sets. Repeat with the remaining shells. To scent, add 2 or 3 drops of scented oil to the wax before it sets. Once the candles have cooled, snip off the excess wicks to ½ inch.

A nice touch is to decorate your shell candles with pearls by pressing the pearls into the surface of the wax, not too near the wick.

CANOPY NOT ONLY protects you from the sun, it creates a private space. And because it's just a ceiling, this space seems both limitless and intimate, especially if you add chairs and a table or maybe two lounging chairs. A canopy is an extremely practical structure, because all you have to do, once you're ready to leave your hideaway in the woods or your vantage point on the beach, is roll it up, tuck it under your arm, and head for home.

The simplest canopy is just a canvas drop cloth, punctuated along all sides with grommets. Using slender rope or clothesline, tie your canopy to four tree trunks, then throw down a blanket and some pillows, and stretch out. If you can't find four trees accommodatingly close together, it's easy to set up a canopy with poles or on the side of a wall. Use an outbuilding wall, apartment wall, or garage wall as a backdrop to your private world.

Project

CANOPY

To make a canopy that attaches to the side of a wall, you
will need:

> *canvas, preferably striped (7 x 8 ½ feet) in a*
>
> > *light or medium weight*
>
> *grommets*
>
> *2 hooks*
>
> *2 5-foot-tall wooden poles*
>
> *nails*
>
> *hammer*
>
> *clothesline*
>
> *2 wooden stakes*

You can purchase canvas at a sailmaker's or awning shop.
Have the shop (or an upholsterer) attach grommets to the four
corners; you may also want to have the shop scallop one edge of
the canopy for decoration. Measure the length between the two
corner grommets on one side of the 7-foot width of canvas, and
affix the two hooks to the wall to the same measurement.
Drive the nails into the tops of the two wooden poles so they
stand out ½ inch, and place 6¾ feet apart so the canvas stays

taut; the distance from the wall should be 8 feet so that the canopy doesn't sag. Once the awning is hooked to the wall and to the poles, tie 7 feet of clothesline to each nail in the pole at one end and a stake at the other. Drive each stake into the ground for anchoring.

For a free-standing canopy, you will need:

4 5-foot-tall wooden poles

4 nails

4 8-foot lengths of clothesline

4 stakes

Drive nails into the tops of all four poles and tie a length of clothesline to each nail at one end. Make four holes in the ground 6 inches deep, making a 7-foot by 7-foot square. Position a stake 2 feet from each pole and tie the clothesline to each stake to stabilize the poles and canopy. Place the canopy atop the poles and position nails in the grommets.

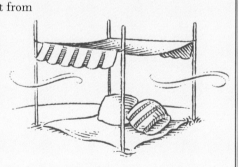

Make a Floral Ice Bucket and Ice Cubes

IFE SEEMS SIMPLER in the summer—maybe because the heat forces us to slow down and relax a little. Even entertaining seems less structured: on a warm summer night you can just ask a few friends over, prop open the back door, set out some comfortable chairs on your deck or patio, and serve up a happy assortment of cool drinks and snacks. For a quick and pretty flourish, make a floral ice bucket for chilling wine, or an iced bowl for serving shrimp, condiments, or punch. Or freeze smaller flowers in ice cubes to brighten glasses of iced lemonade and tea. Your guests will be charmed by how festive this simple arrangement looks—and, what's more, you won't have to worry about your flowers wilting in the heat.

Project

ICE BUCKET

> *5-quart plastic bucket*
>
> *water*
>
> *2-liter plastic soda bottle*
>
> *marbles or gravel*
>
> *selection of flowers and leafy stems*
>
> *towel*
>
> *plate or tray*

Suitable flowers include roses, daisies, pansies, phlox, nasturtiums, marigolds, violas, oxalis, asters, and bachelor's buttons. Fill the bucket half full with tap water and let it stand overnight to disperse the air bubbles. Cut off the top third of the soda bottle, and fill it with marbles or gravel to weight it down. Place it in the water. Drop the flowers into the water and arrange them around the soda bottle. Place the bucket in the freezer. To prevent them from floating to the top, reposition the flowers every hour or so until the water is frozen. Freeze until solid. When you are ready to remove the ice from the bucket, run hot tap water inside the soda bottle and remove first. Then run hot water around the outside of the bucket and release it onto a towel. Place on a plate or tray, and store in the freezer until ready to use. The ice bucket will last about 3 hours in the open air; be sure to keep a tray or plate underneath to catch melting water.

For an ice bowl: Arrange the flowers as above in a clear glass bowl, and freeze until solid. Using hot tap water, remove the ice from the bowl. Arrange condiments or shrimp in the bowl and serve.

For ice cubes: Use smaller flowers (violas, oxalis, nasturtiums, asters, or marigolds) and arrange in water-filled ice cube trays. Freeze the cubes overnight and serve in glasses filled with tea, lemonade, or carbonated water.

AMPERING YOURSELF is essential, even in the lazy days of summer, and if you can splurge on bath oils and bath salts, then you are pampering yourself properly. Making your own bath recipes is simple and particularly satisfying because you can blend the oils to suit—or to counteract—your every mood. A few drops of jasmine oil or sandalwood will reduce anxiety; lavender is calming as well as soothing to the skin; lemon refreshes; and orange awakens creativity. Rose promotes feelings of happiness, while rosemary invigorates and "opens" the heart.

Project

AROMATIC BATH SALTS

> *2-quart mixing bowl*
>
> *2 cups borax*
>
> *⅛ cup French white clay (available at drug, health food,*
>   *or herbalist stores)*
>
> *⅛ cup sea salt*
>
> *wire whisk*
>
> *3 tablespoons essential oil of choice*
>
> *paste food color (optional)*
>
> *toothpick*
>
> *2 8-ounce widemouthed jars with cork or glass stoppers*

All ingredients are available in health food stores or at herbalist shops.

In a 2-quart mixing bowl, mix the dry ingredients using a wire whisk. Make a well in the center of the combined ingredients, and add 1 ½ tablespoons of essential oil. If you are coloring the salts, dab the food color on the end of a toothpick and mix it in. Whisk again to break up clumps and to even out the color. Test the scent and add more oil if desired—

because scent dissipates over time, it's a good idea to add about half again as much oil. Leave uncovered to dry overnight. Spoon into widemouthed jars. Pour a few tablespoons into the bath just as it is filling.

Makes 2 cups

For an energizing bath, add these ingredients to the basic recipe:

10 drops basil oil

9 drops rosemary oil

8 drops coriander oil

6 drops peppermint oil

5 drops ginger oil

4 drops ylang-ylang oil

O RESTORE YOURSELF during the heat of summer, make a refreshing iced tea sorbet garnished with mint blossoms. Mint is a hardy herb with a refreshing flavor that goes excellently with meat or chocolate and also wakens custards, jellies, breads, desserts, teas, even vegetables. Use the entire blossom in this sorbet. Though any kind of mint will do, apple mints, orange mints, peppermints, and spearmints are especially summery.

Project

ICED TEA AND MINT SORBET

20 mint florets, plus extras for garnish	½ cup sugar
1 quart boiling water	tea strainer
4 teaspoons black tea or 4 tea bags	3 tablespoons lemon juice
	ice cream maker
	lemons for garnish

First, rinse the mint blossoms and pat dry. Use the whole flower as a garnish or strip the individual florets from the stems. If you are mixing the mint with fruit, you may wish to crush the florets to disperse the flavor.

Brew a pot of tea (try combining spicy flavors such as Darjeeling, Earl Grey, and orange pekoe) and add the blossoms along with the sugar. Steep for 20 minutes. Strain the tea to remove the blossoms and tea leaves. Let the tea stand until it reaches room temperature.

Add the lemon juice, and refrigerate until cold. Pour the cold tea into an ice cream maker and process according to the manufacturer's instructions.

For fluffy sorbet, let the mixture sit for a few minutes and then run it briefly through a food processor just before serving. Scoop it into slender glasses, and garnish with blossoms and lemon slices. This sorbet is particularly good with ginger cookies.

Makes 1 quart

PRESSING FLOWERS may seem like a pastime of the idle, but documenting plants you have collected from your garden or on a trip isn't as frivolous as you might think. Remember that Captain Cook, on his 18th-century voyages through the Pacific, pressed plants that now provide a crucial clue to long-gone flora; and in the 1800s explorer John Charles Fremont came back from the American West with a cache of pressed plants that detailed the abundance of the frontier. Encourage young modern-day explorers to keep track of a summer trip or stay at camp with a journal of pressed flowers—sorted, dated, and labeled—as a fond reminder of a special summer. Or mount and frame the flowers, and display them individually or in groups.

If you want to experiment in your own yard first, start with your favorite flower bed and gather the first blooms of each plant: pansies, nasturtiums, violas, and daisies.

Project

PRESSED FLOWER COLLECTION

plants, leaves, and bark of your choice

small knife

newsprint paper

blotting paper

corrugated cardboard

flower press or heavy book

waxed paper

white glue

frames, if framing

a journal, if you are documenting your collection

You may want to gather all of the plant; even roots, when cleaned, can look wonderfully artistic when pressed. If the plant is too large for the page in your journal or the paper you are pressing it with, fold it over—this also looks graceful when preserved.

For trees and shrubs, pick the ends of the branch and some bark. Clean the plant by hand to remove the soil. If the root is thick and you want to preserve it too, cut it in half lengthwise with a small knife. Position the specimen at one end of a wide sheet of newsprint, and fold the paper over on top of the plant (use blank paper for white flowers). Place thick blotting paper on either side of the newsprint and a corrugated cardboard layer on either side of the blotting paper. Use a flower press or a heavy book (if using a phone book, substitute a paper towel for newsprint). Label and date. Close the book and place it in a dry, ventilated spot for several days. For succulents, replace the blotting paper daily. For delicate flowers, place waxed paper on top to keep them from sticking to the blotting paper.

INFORMALITY RULES in summer, particularly at big family get-togethers on the Fourth of July and Labor Day. It even seems that everyone's favorite picnic foods—fried chicken, pickles, popcorn, corn on the cob, hamburgers, and hot dogs—are best eaten with the hands. If you're looking for outsized napkins to thrust at enthusiastic and messy gourmands, remember that plain white dishcloths are big enough to drape over an entire lap and generous enough to wipe off lots of little hands. Make these utilitarian cloths distinctive by having them professionally monogrammed, or give them a particularly summery treatment by applying leaf impressions. Using a hammer and your favorite leaves (or at least those with interesting shapes, such as ferns and geraniums), you can achieve an imprint that will survive numerous washings and ironings. Eventually the green color will fade to a delicate brown, and this fragile shading has its own appeal.

Project

SUMMER NAPKINS

heavy paper, such as Kraft paper

cotton or linen dishcloths

selection of green leaves

hammer

Spread a piece of heavy paper (Kraft paper is available at most craft stores) onto a smooth surface. Place a cotton or linen cloth on top and position the leaves as desired on the cloths. Place another piece of paper on top of the leaves. Hold the paper securely in place and begin to firmly hammer each leaf, following the leaf's outline. Hammering will release the chlorophyll, which will leave an impression of the leaves on the cloth.

VEN THE MOST spur-of-the-moment event can become festive with these inexpensive slipcovers for standard ladderback chairs. For an informal look, mix and match towels; for a touch of distinction, use fancier linen or damask in a solid color—at night, gleaming damask can look amazingly elegant. And since they are made out of dish towels, they will withstand all the wear and tear that comes with summer entertaining outdoors.

Project

CHAIR SLIPCOVERS

    5 19- x 28-inch cotton or linen dish towels

    matching cotton thread

    iron

    grosgrain ribbon (8 feet per chair)

Select your five towels, and place towel 1 on top of towel 2, right sides together. Sew together the two long sides and one short side, using a ¼-inch seam. With right sides together, sew towel 3 to the remaining short edge of towel 2, using a ¼-inch seam. Press the seam open.

Place right sides of towels 3 and 4 together. Towel 3 will become the seat and front of the slipcover and will fold over the front of the chair. Stitch the short edge of towel 4 to the long edge of towel 3 from A to B. Pivot, and stitch from B to C. Stitch towel 5 to the opposite edge of towel 3, following the same instructions. Press the seams open. Turn the slipcover right-side out.

Lap the free edge of towel 1 over the edge of towel 4, which is right next to it. Top-stitch from C to D. Cut the grosgrain ribbon into 48-inch segments, two per chair. Machine-stitch the end of one tie to towel 4 just below C. Machine-stitch the end of the second tie to corner of towel 5 at E. Turn the free ends under and stitch a ¼-inch hem. Place the slipcover on chair, and tie closed.

Tip: For a more tailored and well-finished look, iron each seam as you sew it, then iron again when you have completed the slipcover.

Makes 1 slipcover

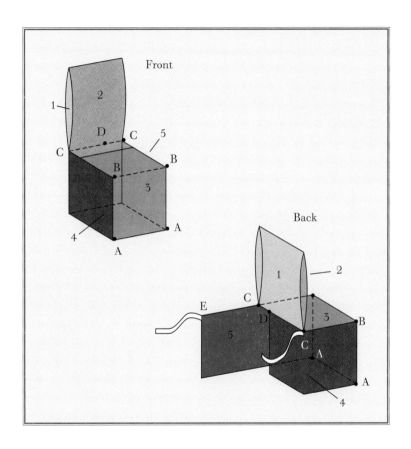

Front

1
2
D   C   5
C   B
B
3
4   A
A

Back

1   2
C   3   B
E
D
5   C   A
4   A

37

ORCHES AND DECKS are especially inviting in summer, particularly if they're painted in crisp white, sunny yellow, or sky blue. Indoors, painted floors can be just as eye-catching, though perhaps unexpectedly so. If you think a patterned floor might give a dull room added dimension, try outsized squares in different colors or a tailored border in a contrasting shade. Or if you're aiming for a dramatic backdrop for your furnishings, opt for a solid color such as elegant white, daring black, or vibrant red. Either way, painting your floors is an easy and inexpensive method of hiding any imperfections and giving your rooms a new lease on life.

Project

FLOOR PAINTING

grid paper

220-grade sandpaper

sanding blocks

several large-bristle brushes

primer paint

painter's tape

wax-pencil china marker

glossy enamel paint in

 desired color

clear sealer

If you are planning to paint a patterned floor, make a scale drawing of the room on the grid paper. Next, remove all the furniture and prepare the floor: lightly sand the floor with 220-grade paper to remove the old wax, or rent an electric sander if you have a large space to cover. Damp mop and sweep to remove dust. Paint with a base color or primer, and let dry. If you are making a pattern, lay it out with painter's tape at this point and use your china marker if necessary (pencil marks will show through the paint). With your pattern in place, apply a second coat of paint, this time using a glossy enamel. Use three coats if the wood floor is freshly sanded; two coats if it is already painted. Seal with clear sealer.

To paint a border or stripes: Measure the width of each stripe on the floor and mark it with painter's tape. Paint between the tape and about ½ inch over the edge. Remove the tape, and let the stripes or border dry. Repeat as necessary.

OME THINGS ARE so commonplace, they are practically invisible. Rope, for instance, is such a practical item that the beauty of its coarse, sinuous texture largely goes unappreciated. This summer, brighten a corner of your favorite room with a rope lamp. Wrap a plain lamp base with rope, then add a parchment or linen shade to filter the light softly. You'll find that even rope can be expressive when used in an unusual way.

Project
ROPE LAMP

> *100 feet of 3-ply rope*
>
> *inexpensive lamp with a large, bulbous base*
>
> *¾-inch flat brush*
>
> *heavy-duty, all-purpose glue*

Manila, jute, or sisal rope are all suitable and can be purchased at hardware or marine supply shops. To make sure that you have enough rope, first coil it completely around the lamp base. With a small, flat brush, apply the glue from the bottom of the lamp up, one 6-inch section at a time. Begin coiling the rope from the bottom, pressing it to the glue and holding it in place until the glue begins to set (about 10 seconds). Continue coiling, pressing each row of rope firmly against the one below it so that there are no gaps. Apply the glue and rope as needed, until you reach the top of the lamp base; then trim the end of the rope on an angle and tuck it underneath the last coil.

TENCILING IS AN EASY, versatile, and inexpensive method of embellishing walls, floors, cabinets, trays, boxes, and anything else that stands still. The technique probably dates back to the Middle Ages and may actually have been invented in France, for it is the French word *estanceler* ("to sparkle" or "to cover with stars") which gives this craft its name. Why not take the French at their word this summer and make a tray stenciled with stars for serving evening drinks?

The Victorians made their stencils from zinc so that they would last, but cardboard will do just as well. Don't worry about technique; precision is nice, but even a casual application of paint can achieve a delightful effect. There is only one rule to stenciling: Don't cover your paintbrush with lots of paint. A nearly dry brush with a light application of paint yields the best results.

Project

STAR-STENCILED TRAY

> *manila paper*
>
> *tracing paper*
>
> *pencil*
>
> *small craft knives for cutting the stencil*
>
> *tray (any kind will do)*
>
> *short-bristle brushes*
>
> *quick-drying artists' acrylic paint*
>
> *plastic lids on which to mix paints (optional)*

Select your star design and trace it onto the manila paper; if you are a confident artist, draw your design directly onto the paper. Cut out the stencil with a small craft knife (a cheap one works very well for this project) by moving the knife toward you. Don't worry about the quality of the cut edge since stencils tend to be fuzzy anyway. Plan out the pattern on another sheet of paper or just lay the stencil randomly on the tray (clean the tray thoroughly and let dry before painting). Apply color (mix paints on a plastic lid until the desired color is achieved) to a brush, being careful not to overload the brush. Wipe off the surplus paint, and dampen the brush slightly with water if it is dry.

Paint through the cut-out part of the stencil, using circular strokes and building up the color. Use a separate brush for each color. When two colors overlap, merge them to achieve a third color. It's okay to lift the corner of the stencil to check on the effect you are creating. Never worry about mistakes when stenciling—they are part of the charm of this unpretentious undertaking.

OUR GRANDMOTHERS made jams, jellies, preserves, conserves, marmalades, and fruit butters as part of their weekly routine. The delectable results, which we may have forgotten, make grocery store concoctions pale in comparison. Preparing jellies isn't a difficult process, and it is a way to preserve summer fruits for year-round enjoyment. Homemade jellies are also wonderful holiday and hostess gifts during the winter months. This lemon-lime marmalade (different from a jelly in that it contains little bits of the fruit) is a sprightly spread for hot buttered biscuits, as well as a refreshing condiment with meats.

Project

LEMON-LIME MARMALADE

You probably already own most of the equipment you will
need to make your marmalade:

*large stainless steel or heavy
aluminum cooking pot
(large enough to hold
three times the fruit being
used) with lid*

quart-size Mason jars

large pot for sterilizing jars

*rack to place in bottom of
large pot while
sterilizing jars*

jar lifter

a clean towel

jar lids and rings

*small saucepan for
sterilizing jar caps
and rings*

*assortment of small
utensils: a wooden spoon
for stirring, a paring
knife, measuring cups
and spoons, a slotted
spoon, a ladle*

For the marmalade,
you will need:

5 large limes

5 lemons (same size as limes)

sugar as needed

Slice fruit thin and remove the seeds. Put the sliced fruit into a large cooking pot and add enough water to just cover the fruit. Cover the pot and cook fruit until the rinds are tender. Measure the fruit and liquid with a measuring cup and stir in an equal amount of sugar. Boil the mixture rapidly until the liquid reaches the setting point of jelly. (The best way to recognize the setting point is to ladle up some of the juice in a spoon, let it cool slightly, and let it fall back into the pan. If the juice forms two drops that run together and fall off the spoon in a sheet, the jelly is ready.)

Sterilize jars ahead of time to be ready for filling. Boil for 10 minutes and then let them sit in the hot water. Just before marmalade is ready, remove jars with the jar lifter, shake off excess water, and place on a clean towel to drain. Follow the same procedure with the jar lids. Ladle the marmalade into jars, leaving ¼ inch of space between the liquid and top of the jar. Wipe off any spillage, especially from the threads at the mouths of the jars. Seal tightly by hand. Turn jar upside down and hold a few seconds so that the hot liquid covers the sides of the jar (this helps destroy bacteria). Place the jars in a boiling water bath with water 2 inches above the jar tops and at least 1 inch of space between the jars. Cover, and boil for 10 minutes. Remove and let cool. Check lids to see that they have sunk down, indicating an airtight seal. Store in cool, dark, dry place.

Makes 1 jar of marmalade

OST OF US MANAGE to slip away for at least a few weeks during the summer. If we're lucky, it's to a place we love and visit again and again: a cabin in the mountains, a cottage by the sea, a house next to a meadow. Make your hideaway really feel like home by adding a few simple and inexpensive touches such as painted floors, big chairs for flopping into, and café curtains handmade from vintage linens (often embroidered and of better quality material than new tea towels). Café curtains hit a window at its midpoint, letting light flood in at the top but filter in at the bottom; they also allow for privacy without shutting you completely away from the world. Old tea towels usually fit half a window exactly, so you only need to do the simplest cutting and sewing to make elegant curtains that waft gently in the breeze.

Project

CAFÉ CURTAINS

> *vintage linen tea towels*
>
> *curtain rods (brass is best with this look)*
>
> *needle*
>
> *matching curtain rings, clip- or sew-on*
>
> *cotton thread*

Cut the tea towel in half across the width: if the towel has embroidered ends, these will be the bottom borders of each curtain. Hang the curtain rod midway in the window. Make a ½-inch hem at the top (and bottom, if necessary) of the curtains. Attach the curtain rings. If you are using clip-on rings, clip at 3-inch intervals. Otherwise, sew curtain rings on at desired intervals using matching thread. If you prefer not to use rings at all, make the hem generous enough to insert the curtain rod; gather the curtain across the rod and hang.

OOLING YOUR HEELS in a summer stream can offer instant refreshment, as well as the chance to relax and savor the moment. You can hold onto that moment by taking home pleasing pebbles you find in the streambed and writing an evocative word on each one—"rain," "joy," "smile," "touch"—that works singly or in combination to express a special sentiment. Keep your collection in a pretty bowl or basket by a sunny window or next to a comfortable armchair, so that you can look at the pebbles or even pick them up whenever you need reminding of what's important in your life. Buffed and buffeted by the water for eons, these smooth little rocks testify to the magic of endurance.

Project

POETRY PEBBLES

pebbles, any size

eyeliner brush or Japanese calligraphy brush

acrylic paint in desired colors

fine-line permanent black marker

fine-line gold marker

acrylic spray varnish

Wash the pebbles thoroughly, and let dry. Write your words of choice on them with a liner brush and paint or with fine-line markers. Add illustrations or symbols, too. Let the pebbles dry overnight, then spray them with acrylic varnish, and let dry.

You can apply the same technique to larger rocks and stones, then scatter them throughout your garden.

F YOUR EYES FEEL TIRED or irritated this summer, make an eye compress from clary sage, which has cooling, soothing properties. Even its name—"clear-eye" in old English—suggests a long history of healing eye problems. Clary sage is also used as an ingredient in cologne and toilet water and is even a component of vermouth and some wines. The essential oil is available at herb shops and health food stores; be sure to ask for clary sage, which is different from the more common variety of sage.

Project

CLEAR-EYE COMPRESS

small saucepan

water

small container

7 to 10 drops of clary sage essential oil

cotton balls

Boil 2 cups of water in a small saucepan and then let it cool slightly. Pour 1 cup of the hot water into a small container or cup. Add 7 to 10 drops of clary sage oil to the water, then soak a cotton ball in the mixture and gently squeeze out any excess. Place a compress over each eye and relax for 10 minutes.

Makes 1 cup

BEFORE SUNTANNED SKIN became fashionable, women took pride in the creaminess of their complexions, which they carefully protected by wearing large-brimmed hats or carrying parasols. Today it's acknowledged that a suntan only conveys the appearance of good health, and that it's best to cover up and stay out of the sunlight. A charming summer hat that flutters in the wind and creates teasing shadows is still one of the best and most attractive ways of guarding your face against ultraviolet rays. So make a hat for summertime, and make it fanciful: ribbons and roses on your bonnet are the height of fashion, and also a cheerful gesture to everyone who sees you.

SUMMER HAT

> *wide-brimmed straw hat*
>
> *wire-edged ribbon in same shade (3 ¼ feet long x*
>   *3 inches wide)*
>
> *matching thread*
>
> *needle*
>
> *a selection of wire-edged ribbons in other colors (20 inches*
>   *long and 1 ½ inches wide) or silk roses from a craft shop*
>
> *bronze or light green ribbon (3 ½ feet)*

Sew the wide ribbon around the bottom of the hat's crown with tiny, widely spaced stitches. Tie the ribbon ends into a bow. To make a ribbon rose, select a length of ribbon and hold down one end of the wire that runs through one edge. Pull the ribbon along this wire and gather tightly. Fold the end of the ribbon over, and turn the gathered ribbon around on itself to form the shape of a flower. Use the drawn-up wire that remains to wrap around the base of the ribbon rose. Make rose leaves by cutting green or bronze ribbon into 6-inch pieces. Find the midpoint of one side of the 6-inch length, and fold the top edge on either side of the midpoint

down over the ribbon. Turn over the ribbon, and fold the
edges to the middle. Stitch closed and attach to a ribbon rose.
Sew roses and leaves to the back of the hat next to the bow.

I'T'S HARD TO RESIST picking up seashells as you stroll along the beach, and it's worth keeping in mind that you can actually make something from your collection. Framed seashell pictures, also called "sailor's valentines," were very fashionable in Victorian times, as was the craft of making boxes decorated with shells. You too can create your own boxes with shell lids, either for keeping your own treasures in or for giving away as gifts with little trinkets nestled inside.

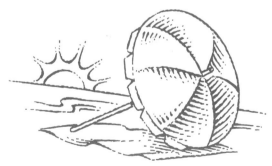

Project

SEASHELL KEEPSAKE BOX

small wooden boxes	*selection of shells*
paint in desired color	*PVA glue*
fine sandpaper	*tweezers*
rags	*paper lace*
gilt cream	

Using fine sandpaper, lightly sand the wooden boxes (available in various shapes from craft shops) and wipe off the dust. Apply two coats of paint and let dry completely. Using a rag, rub the gilt cream (also available at craft stores) over the sides of the box and the edge of the lid. Polish with a clean rag. Select the shells and arrange them on the lid to test your design, then remove them. Apply the glue in a spiral around the lid of the box, and position the shells on the lid with tweezers. Be sure to pack them tightly together. Finish the box with a strip of lace around its base and the bottom edge of the lid.

UMMER OFTEN MEANS a long-anticipated getaway to a beach house or mountain cabin, where you've accumulated happy memories in slow time. Perhaps summer retreats seem so enjoyably uncomplicated because furnishings are pared down and housekeeping kept to a minimum. Add a carefree touch to your bedroom with an ingenious headboard made from fence pickets—a whimsical allusion to cottages and little gardens that fits in nicely with your back-to-basics summer lifestyle.

Project

PICKET HEADBOARD

> *a section of picket fencing in your choice of style*
>
> *sandpaper*
>
> *sanding block*
>
> *sponge brushes*
>
> *latex flat paint*
>
> *matte finish sealer*
>
> *short nails*
>
> *heavy-gauge braided picture wire*
>
> *2 100-pound picture hangers*
>
> *hammer*
>
> *crackle-finish kit (optional)*

You will need 39 inches of a length of fencing for a single bed, 54 inches for a double, 60 inches for a queen, and 78 inches for a king-size bed.

Sand the fence and wipe off any excess dust. With a sponge brush, apply the first coat of paint, which will act as the primer. Sand again for a uniform finish. Apply the second coat of paint and let dry. Finally, apply the sealer. To anchor the headboard, attach two short nails to the back of the next-to-last picket at each end of the fencing. The nails should be next to each other and about 2 inches apart, depending on the width of the pickets (see diagram below). Wrap the braided picture wire around the nails to create hangers, and hang the fence on picture hangers as you would a picture.

If you want to apply a crackle-finish, begin the process after the first coat of paint is applied, which should show through the cracks in the finish. Apply the topcoat while the paint is still wet, making sure your coverage is consistent. The topcoat can only be applied once. Let dry for at least a day.

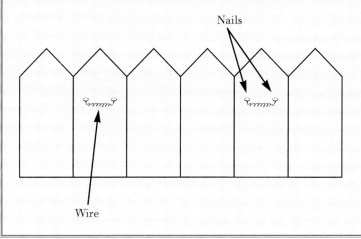

Nails

Wire

SUNBURN USED TO BE regarded as part and parcel of a summer's day spent outdoors. Though today its dangers are well known, it's not always possible to avoid overexposure to the sun. So if you're suffering from too much sun, it's worth remembering that the oil derived from patchouli—a member of the lavender family—acts as a sedative when mixed in a warm bath and has anti-inflammatory properties that soothe sunburned skin. The musky scent of patchouli became very fashionable during the Victorian era, when cashmere shawls were shipped from India to Britain packed in patchouli leaves to repel moths—though no doubt rumors that the plant was an aphrodisiac also boosted its popularity!

Project
PATCHOULI BATH SOAK

almond oil

patchouli oil

Mix 10 drops of each oil in a warm bath to soothe burned skin and release tension.

THE BALMIER WEATHER naturally invites you to stretch out on a blanket and gaze at the night-time skies—and these are at their most glorious on August 11 each year, when the Perseid meteoric showers swarm throughout the heavens. First sighted nearly 2,000 years ago by the Chinese, this spectacular display is best observed away from the lights of towns. Take a friend and a picnic with you, as well as lots of wishes to make on all the shooting stars you're bound to see. Some say the best way to view a shooting star is to frame it with your hands as it streaks across the sky.

Project

MAKE A WISH

Recite this wish out loud as soon as you sight your star:

"Star light, star bright,

First star I see tonight.

Wish I may,

Wish I might,

Have the wish I wish tonight."

After you've made your wish, don't look back at the star—and, if you really want to make sure your wish comes true, don't speak until you see another shooting star.

Make a Leafy Lamp Shade

EAVES ARE AT THEIR PROUDEST during the glory days of summer, when they seem to exist solely to make our lives shadier, cooler, and prettier. In fact, midsummer is the best time to gather up and preserve some of your favorite leaves, perhaps to use as decorations. Try decorating a plain paper lamp shade with leaf imprints: it's a delightful way to remind yourself of summer all year round.

Project

LEAF LAMP SHADE

fleshy leaves (such as magnolia, willow, or eucalyptus)

several bowls filled with water

soft paintbrush

iron

heavy book for pressing the leaves

white or off-white paper lamp shade

glue

lamp base

Use leaves from your own garden or purchase them from a florist. Look for various shapes and sizes; if you want predictable results, choose leaves with perfect shapes. Soak your collection in a bowl of water—rainwater is a delightful organic option—for about a month (change the water weekly) to soften the tissue between the leaf veins. After a month, remove the leaves and rinse them with cold water. Using a soft brush, gently remove the leaf tissue between the veins. Let dry overnight. Iron the leaves on a low setting (it's fine to iron the leaf directly) and place them between the pages of a book to keep them flat until you are ready to use them.

Holding the leaves up to the lamp shade, experiment with your intended design. Next, gently brush the back of one leaf with glue and position it on the shade. Be sure to press each leaf firmly so that it will adhere to the curved surface. Repeat the procedure, maintaining an even space between the leaves, until the lamp shade is covered. Let dry, then place the shade on a lamp base.

ERHAPS BECAUSE DAYLIGHT in the summer is so intense, we tend to want to illuminate the nights softly—with lanterns, strings of lights draped over a porch, and candles. A flickering glow can be very soothing, particularly after a stressful workday or a frustrating traffic jam. For special occasions, why not decorate your plain white candles with dried flowers? Besides being beautiful, candles made with fragrant plants and herbs such as lavender and rosemary will envelope you in a delicate aroma.

Project

FLORAL CANDLES

> *wax glue*
>
> *small double saucepan*
>
> *small soft paintbrush*
>
> *wax candles in various sizes*
>
> *dried flowers, leaves, and herbs*
>
> *3- x 8-inch dipping can (available at craft stores) or any*
>   *aluminum can in the shape you want for your candles*
>
> *2 pounds paraffin wax*
>
> *deep saucepan*

Melt 4 tablespoons of wax glue over hot water in a small double saucepan. With the small paintbrush, dot a candle with glue wherever you want to position the flowers. Press the flowers onto the candle in the desired pattern. Fill the dipping can full of paraffin wax and put into a deep saucepan of nearly boiling water to melt. Hold the candle by its wick and quickly dip it in and out of the hot wax; dip twice only, making sure that the outer layer of wax isn't so thick that the flowers don't show through. Let dry.

Make a Lavender Pomander

NE OF SUMMER'S most fragrant and profuse bloomers is lavender, which for centuries has been used to perfume rooms, closets, chests of drawers, and trunks; the Elizabethans even rubbed their furniture with lavender oil to give it a luxurious sheen. Lavender is also known to have numerous therapeutic properties: its oil helps relieve the distress caused by arthritis, while its aroma can banish headaches, promote tranquility, and induce sleep. So fill your house with lavender, from bowls brimming with dried buds, to baskets of sheaves, to wreaths. It's also easy to make lavender pomanders to use in your linen and clothes closets, or to give away as gifts to friends.

Project

LAVENDER POMANDER

flat bowl or tray

dried lavender flowers

Styrofoam balls

pencil

paintbrush

lavender paint

PVA glue

wire ribbon

Fill a bowl or tray with dried lavender flowers. Pierce a Styrofoam ball with a pencil to use as a handle or to secure the ball while you paint it. With the paintbrush, cover the entire ball with lavender paint to match the flowers. Let dry. Coat the ball with glue and roll it gently in the dried lavender flowers until it is covered. Let dry. Tie the ribbon around the ball twice so that it divides the ball into four quarters. Fill the hole in the top with glue. Wait until the glue is sticky, then with the remaining ribbon, make a bow and push it into the glue-filled hole. For hanging, make another ribbon loop and push the ends into the same hole. Let dry before hanging.

A LAZY SUMMER AFTERNOON filled with the sound of mallets striking wooden balls or the clink of ball against wicket is hard to beat. Croquet is a sport that perfectly suits hot weather: not too fast, not too strenuous, and not too complicated, and it can be played and enjoyed at all levels of competition. The game's devotees include Harpo Marx, who turned a spare bedroom into a closet for all his croquet equipment. Although croquet is considered a daytime game these days, this wasn't always the case, and you can still find old croquet sets with candle attachments on the wickets for nighttime games in some antique stores. Whatever time of day (or night) you play and however strictly (or not) you decide to enforce the rules, you should always follow the tradition of wearing white attire.

Project

CROQUET

The nine-wicket croquet court is a rectangle whose length is
twice its width—50 feet by 100 is recommended. (See diagram.) Mark boundaries with cord and flags, and set up the
wickets (iconoclasts can experiment with a challenging pattern). The blue ball always starts the game, followed by red,
black, and yellow. Making your shot is a lot like putting in golf:
determine where you want your ball to go, and aim carefully.
When you're hitting long shots, the between-the-legs swing is
traditional, but the side swing—as in golf—is more powerful.

To play, place your ball a mallet's length from the starting
stake and try to hit it through the course of wickets. Each
player's turn consists of one stroke. When your ball goes
through the wicket, you get one more stroke, called a continuation stroke. If you hit another ball, you get two strokes. Your
turn lasts as long as you earn continuation strokes. If the ball
hits an opponent's ball, the first player can either hit both
balls (which must be touching each other) in any direction or
the hit ball can be repositioned by placing one foot on the ball
and hitting it with the mallet. The intention here is to send
the opponent's ball in an undesirable direction.

Once you have cleared all the wickets and hit the upper
stake, you are a "rover" and can impede your opponents by

hitting their balls with your own for extra shots. Only when your ball hits the final stake is it removed from play. You earn one point for every wicket you clear and for every stake you strike in the correct order. A game is 32 points.

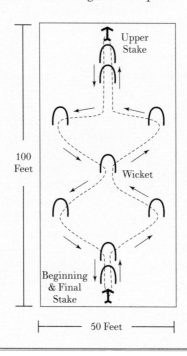

Make a Screen

ALTHOUGH SUMMER encourages you to get away from it all, this may not always be possible, even for a short weekend. But if you are in real need of time to yourself, you can make your own private space with a pretty screen decorated with wallpaper. Place the screen at the end of the bed to create a private nook where you can read and lounge, or set it up on a balcony or patio where it can catch the breeze but block out the sun or intrusions from the outside world. Whenever you don't need the screen, prop it in a corner or use it to take up wasted space in a large room—either way, your screen will provide an eye-catching focal point.

Project

PRIVACY SCREEN

> *3 hollow-core doors*
>
> *sandpaper*
>
> *sanding block*
>
> *primer*
>
> *brush*
>
> *scissors*
>
> *wallpaper (one pattern, mix-and-match, or border print)*
>
> *wallpaper glue (optional)*
>
> *applicator brush for glue or adhesive*
>
> *vinyl-to-vinyl adhesive*
>
> *double-acting hinges*

Sand the doors until they are smooth, then dust off. Paint the doors with primer, and let dry overnight. Follow the manufacturer's application instructions on the wallpaper you select; if glue is necessary, brush it on one side of one door at a time. Cover the front of one door first, wrapping the wallpaper around the sides and to the back. Fold and smooth the

corners as you would wrap a gift. For the back of the door, cut
the paper to the exact size of the door and affix, covering the
folds from the front wallpaper. If you are using a border print,
apply vinyl-to-vinyl adhesive to the front of the wallpaper and
the back of the border print before affixing the border to the
covered door. Repeat with the other panels. Join the panels
with double-acting hinges, three per joint.

Make a Seed Packet

 S YOUR FAVORITE seed-bearing flowers, such as cosmos, marigolds, zinnias, and sunflowers, begin to fade and wither, collect the seeds and set them aside in cardboard packets, marked with their fall planting dates to ensure that you will have more of the same next summer. These little packets also make delightful gifts for friends, who have undoubtedly admired your gardening talents!

Project

tracing paper

pencil

corrugated paper, heavy wrapping paper, kraft paper,
  or lightweight cardboard

scissors

craft or X-acto knife

glue stick

weighty object large enough to press down glued flap

decorative labels (optional)

raffia or twine

ink pen

dried flowers, nuts, acorns, shells (optional)

Trace an envelope shape and folding lines onto tracing paper. With the wrong side of the corrugated paper or cardboard facing you, place your pattern on top and cut out the shape (1). With the tracing paper still in place, prick tiny holes through the cardboard with a pin or the blade point of a craft knife to mark the folding lines. Using the tip of the knife handle, make a deep score along the pricked curved lines and score a line across the center of the envelope. Crease the packet inward along the scored center line.

Fold the long edge inward on the markings and glue the flap (2). Bring the opposite long edge over to meet the glued flap. Place a weight on top and let the glue dry. Then gently squeeze the sides of the packet to open (3) one of the ends with the pricked curves, and fold the flaps along the scored lines. With a pen or pencil, write the contents and planting date on a decorative label and affix, or record your information directly on the packet. Insert the seeds, tie the packet closed with raffia or twine (4), and embellish with dried flowers, nuts, or shells— using the seed's flowers is a particularly nice touch.

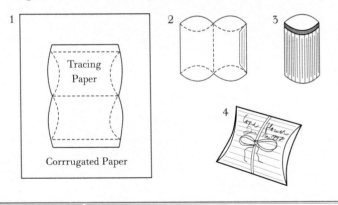

Plant a Potager Garden

ITY-DWELLERS NEEDN'T be deprived of the pleasures of eating garden-fresh vegetables. In fact, it can be easier to grow vegetables in a small city garden, where you can control factors such as soil conditions, weeds, and water much more efficiently than you can in a large garden outdoors. Another plus is that you may not have to use as many pesticides, since a potager garden (full of potted plants) conveniently situated just outside a kitchen or patio door is usually within easy surveillance range.

Remember that vegetable blossoms can be at least as lovely as conventional flowers and will do nicely for decoration—think of the monarchical purple cabbage or the demure squash. But don't forget to include a few flowers, too: pansies, marigolds, and nasturtiums make wonderful salads and garnishes, and they look delightful frozen in ice cubes for tea or lemonade.

Project

POTAGER GARDEN

> *seeds or young plants*
>
> *good soil*
>
> *terra-cotta pots*
>
> *wood, wire, or flexible branches, such as willow,*
>   *for handmade trellises for vines*

Vegetables, flowers, herbs, and fruits that do well in pots include artichokes, beets, onions, lettuce, cabbages, radicchio, peppers, cucumbers, squash, and tomatoes (cherry and plum as well as regular); pansies, marigolds, and nasturtiums (these like poor soil); bay laurel, thyme, parsley, cilantro, mint, basil, rosemary, and dill; and strawberries.

Use various shapes of pots: long rectangular ones for a row of lettuce; big round ones for a grouping of tall herbs, cabbages, and pansies; or pocketed pots with baby lettuce in each pocket. Smaller pots can hold herbs. And be creative— make a little dome for vines to grow through by pushing the ends of willow branches into the dirt around the rim of your pot; or add latticework on one side for a tiny trellis.

HANKS TO ALL the fragrant soaps, lotions, and perfumes we use today, bees, wasps, and mosquitoes find us quite irresistible. If you automatically begin to slap and wave insects off as soon as you get outside, try using a natural insect repellent, one that smells good to people but not to pests. Here's a remedy for bugs that sting; you can also use it on damp hair as a tingling scalp tonic.

Project

INSECT REPELLENT

> *5 drops tea tree oil*
>
> *5 drops eucalyptus oil*
>
> *⅓ cup pure alcohol*
>
> *⅓ cup castor oil*
>
> *small saucepan*
>
> *pitcher or jar (for scalp tonic)*

Mix the ingredients in a small saucepan. Warm the mixture over low heat, being careful not to let it get too hot. Rub it over your skin just before going out.

If you decide to use this recipe on your scalp, first pour the mixture into a pitcher or jar, then over your damp hair. Massage it in, wrap a towel around your head, and wait 10 minutes before rinsing it out.

Make Lavender-Scented Coat Hangers

OU CAN KEEP your clothes fresh and fragrant all summer long with old-fashioned, easy-to-make hangers padded with lavender sachets. What more pleasant experience than opening your closet door to the subtle and lilting aroma of lavender?

Project
QUILTED COAT HANGERS

2 wire coat hangers

20 inches silk or
    lightweight brocade

scissors

10 inches quilted
    polyester padding

2 fistfuls dried lavender flowers

pins

needle

thread

2 feet of cotton lace trim

24 inches of silk wired ribbon

Place a coat hanger on the silk, and cut a length that is double the length of the hanger and 3½ inches wide. Cut the padding slightly longer than the hanger, and wrap around the hanger so that the top part remains open. Distribute the dried lavender throughout the padding, and then sew closed. Place the padded hanger inside the cut silk, and turn the hem under ½ inch. Cut a 24-inch length of lace and insert it between the seam around the hanger. Pin and hand-stitch closed, beginning on one side of the crook and ending on the other side. Bind the crook with ribbon, and tie in a bow.

Makes 2 hangers

Paint a Sisal Rug

RING SOME OF THE TEXTURES of summer indoors with a sisal rug, a practical and beautiful way to cover a floor. Made from hardy grasses woven in various textures, sisal rugs provide sturdy surfaces for all sorts of activities—whether they're tossed on a porch, stretched down an entry hall, or laid down in a living or family room. And since these rugs are so inexpensive, why not experiment with painting them? You'll find that even an old or worn sisal rug takes on new life with a painted design of squares, triangles, or something seasonal like flowers and leaves.

Project
SISAL RUG

sisal rug, any size

drop cloth

heavy books

scissors

3-inch-wide masking tape

newspaper or Kraft paper

particle mask

latex gloves

can of interior-exterior spray paint

can of interior-exterior spray paint in contrasting shade

  (optional)

You might want to experiment first with a small bath or welcome mat. Choose a well-ventilated area in which to work—even outdoors if you have enough room. Prepare your work area by spreading a drop cloth on the floor and unrolling your rug. Lay it flat on the drop cloth, and use heavy books as weights if the ends curl. Cut stencils from the masking tape in desired shapes (but don't worry too much about precision). If your shapes are bigger than the masking tape, cut them from newspaper or Kraft paper and tape them to the rug. Press the stenciled tape onto the rug in a pleasing pattern; free-form works well on these casual rugs. If you want the border to be a different color, tape it off now. Put on a mask and gloves. Shake the paint can for 2 minutes longer than is recommended in the manufacturer's instructions. Holding the can about 10 inches from the rug, spray it lightly, making sure you are applying an even coat over the entire rug. Reshake every few minutes. If your coverage is uneven, immediately apply a second coat. Let dry overnight. If you are adding a border in another color, cover the newly sprayed and now dry area of the rug with newspaper and secure with tape. Spray border and let dry overnight. Remove the tape and let the rug air for a few days before setting furniture on it.

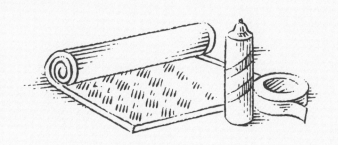

THOUGH WE ASSOCIATE summertime with gardening, in many areas of the country the weather is just too hot to work outside. A water garden requires minimal upkeep, and it can be a charming solution to the difficulties of gardening in small urban spaces. Try a small, single water garden, and then experiment with clustering three or four together. To re-create the soothing sound of a gurgling fountain, install an aquarium bubbler in one of the pots; as in an aquarium, the bubbler will keep the plants aerated and encourage them to flower.

Consider the amount of sunlight your garden will actually get, and purchase your plants accordingly. To minimize the potential for breeding mosquitoes, think about adding goldfish to your pond, but be sure to include oxygenating plants in your scheme to provide a healthy ecosystem for the fish. Also, choose plants of varying heights and textures to create a dramatic look: for example, the tall, reedlike horsetail rush contrasts nicely with pondweed, an oxygenating plant that grows low to the water. Water hawthorn with its fragrant white flowers, yellow iris, Queen of the Nile with its pom-pom of blue blossoms, and the blue-blooming pickerel weed will all add splashes of color to the greenery.

Project

WATER GARDEN

> *waterproof plastic, sealed cement, metal, or ceramic pot*
> *(at least 20 inches deep and 30 inches in diameter)*
> *sand or gravel*
> *tap water*
> *plants*
> *goldfish*

Place about 2 inches of sand or gravel in the bottom of the pot. Fill the pot with tap water and add the plants, pushing them into the sand or gravel to stabilize them. If you are adding goldfish, wait a few days until the plants have begun oxygenating the water (or purchase a bottle of oxygenating solution from a pet store to help the fish adjust).

Make a Hanging Vase

IELD TO SOME of the extravagance of summer—
the enthusiastically blooming flowers, the warm
and sensuous weather, perhaps even some extra
free time. As a happy gesture to neighbors and passersby,
hang a summery vase of flowers on your front door. These
leaf-wrapped containers are so unexpectedly pretty, you
might be tempted to make more than one and decorate a
balcony or outside wall with them.

Project

HANGING VASE

> *large fresh leaves, 4 to 6 inches longer than the vase's height*
>
> *florist's clay*
>
> *old plastic juice containers, drinking glasses, or*
> *widemouthed jars*

---

florist's tape

rubber bands

raffia

seedpods (optional)

flowers

nail

hammer

Choose rubbery leaves (such as magnolia, fig, or loquat) or purchase coconut bark from a craft store. Set aside three strips of florist's clay, and press onto the container just beneath the mouth, around the bottom, and around the middle. Cover the jar with fresh leaves front and back, wrapping from bottom to top. Press the leaves to the clay, and secure. Fold under the stem ends of the back and side leaves to cover the bottom of the container, then secure them with florist's tape or rubber bands. Wrap raffia around the rubber bands to conceal them. Tie off tightly at the front in a bow and add a cluster of seed-pods, or make raffia tassels by knotting the ends and shredding the raffia below the knot. To hang the vase, tie another loop of raffia to each end of the raffia belt, so that it hangs like a purse. Fill the vase with water and flowers—sturdy ones such as sunflowers work best—and hang from a nail on the wall.

Make Sugared Flowers

EMEMBER THE CHARMING candied violets that used to adorn dainty cookies and cakes? Once a commonplace delicacy for tea or dessert, they now seem oddly quaint—though sugared flowers instantly make a plain summer dessert very special. Besides their visual appeal, they offer marvelously subtle flavors. Hyssop tastes like licorice, and borage flowers like cucumbers, while nasturtiums add a peppery zing to salads and meats. Pansies, Johnny-jump-ups, and violets all lend a bit of wintergreen flavor to foods. Marigolds have a flavor reminiscent of saffron.

If you are gathering blossoms from your own garden, pick unblemished ones early in the morning or late in the afternoon the day you are planning to use them. Wash them gently, shake off any excess water, and let them dry on a paper towel. Then place the flowers in a plastic bag and keep them refrigerated until it's time to use them.

Project

SUGARED FLOWERS

2 egg whites (for about 10 blossoms)

tweezers

unblemished blossoms

waxed paper

1 cup sugar (clear or colored)

flour sifter

Whip the egg whites by hand in a bowl until frothy. Using tweezers, dip each flower one by one into the frothy mixture. Place the flowers on a sheet of waxed paper. Put the sugar into the flour sifter and sift it over the flowers, making sure to give them a fine, even coating. Let them dry, and then arrange on top of or around a cake, or use as a garnish for puddings, meats, or cookies. Since the egg whites haven't been cooked, it is best to eat the flowers shortly after making them (but these confections are so irresistible, you won't want to wait long to eat them anyway).

HINK OF THE ENCHANTMENT of sleeping out under the summer sky when you were a child, the stars sprinkled above you. If you have a four-poster bed, you can re-create some of the magic of a starry night in your own bedroom. Get as many strings of tiny white lights as you can find and can afford, and wrap each post of your bed with the strands. If your bed has a canopy, experiment with criss-crossing the strings of lights across the top to make your own private and glittering heaven. But don't despair if your bed lacks posts—you can wrap the headboard in lights, so that your bed resembles an exotic, bright barge that will float you to dreamland every night.